DARKNESS

by Mildred Pitts Walter

Illustrated by Marcia Jameson

Simon & Schuster Books for Young Readers

SIMON & SCHUSTER BOOKS FOR YOUNG READERS
An imprint of Simon & Schuster Children's Publishing Division
1230 Avenue of the Americas, New York, New York 10020
Text copyright © 1995 by Mildred Pitts Walter
Illustrations copyright © 1995 by Marcia Jameson
All rights reserved including the right of
reproduction in whole or in part in any form.
SIMON & SCHUSTER BOOKS FOR YOUNG READERS
is a trademark of Simon & Schuster.
Book design by Julie Y. Quan and Carolyn Boschi.
The text of this book is set in 18 point Galliard.
The illustrations are rendered in acrylic.
Manufactured in Hong Kong by
South China Printing Company (1988) Ltd.
First edition
1 2 3 4 5 6 7 8 9 10
LIBRARY OF CONGRESS CATALOGING-IN-PUBLICATION DATA
Walter, Mildred Pitts.
Darkness / by Mildred Pitts Walter;
illustrated by Marcia Jameson. — 1st ed.
p. cm.
Summary: A celebration of the many
wonderful things that flourish in darkness.
ISBN 0-689-80305-2
[1. Shades and shadows—Fiction. 2. Night—Fiction.]
I. Jameson, Marcia, ill. II. Title.
PZ7.W17125Dar 1995 [E]—dc20 94-15264

For Irma, Jewel, and Johari

M. P. W.

Dedicated to my daughters,
Kim and Tien

M. J.

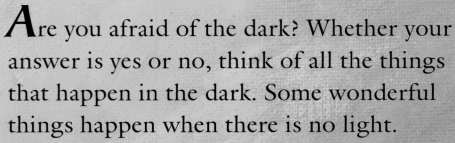

Are you afraid of the dark? Whether your answer is yes or no, think of all the things that happen in the dark. Some wonderful things happen when there is no light.

    The fiery falling star and pinpoint lights, far away in the sky, can only be seen in the dark.

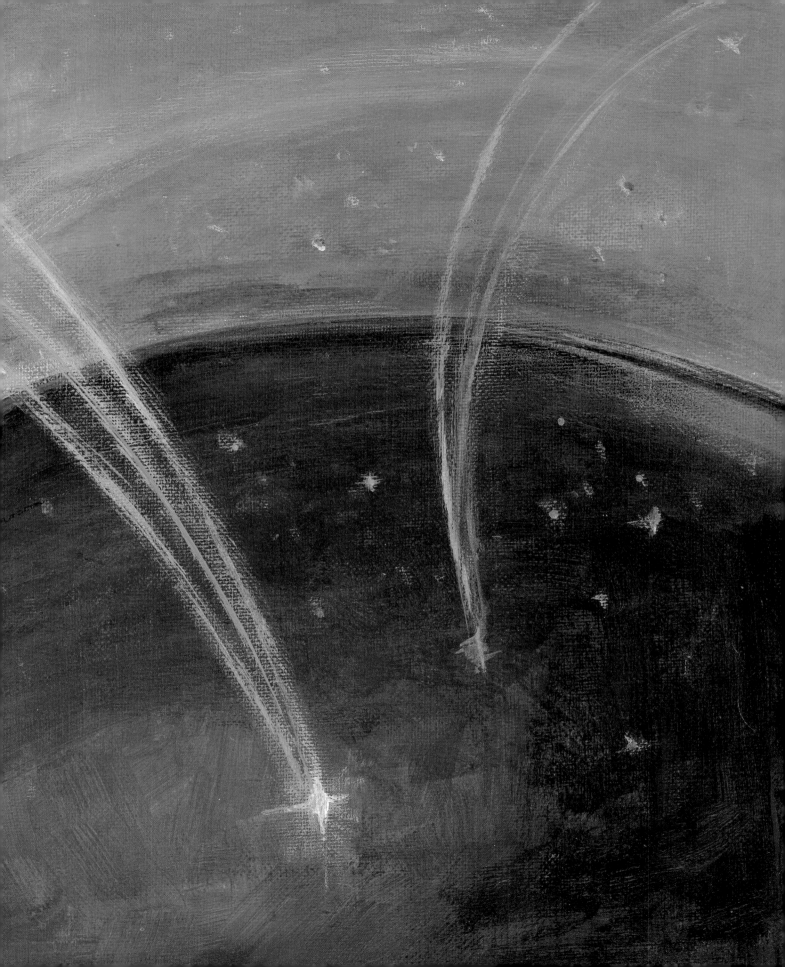

Life begins in the darkness: Babies begin in the darkness of their mothers' wombs.

Seeds become plants
in the darkness of
the earth.

Gold, silver, sparkling diamonds…all
are formed in dark seams of the earth.

Many plants and animals live together
in the deep, dark waters of the sea.

Dark clouds bring refreshing rain. It seeps down into the earth and returns, bubbling up from the darkness, crystal clear in the light of day.

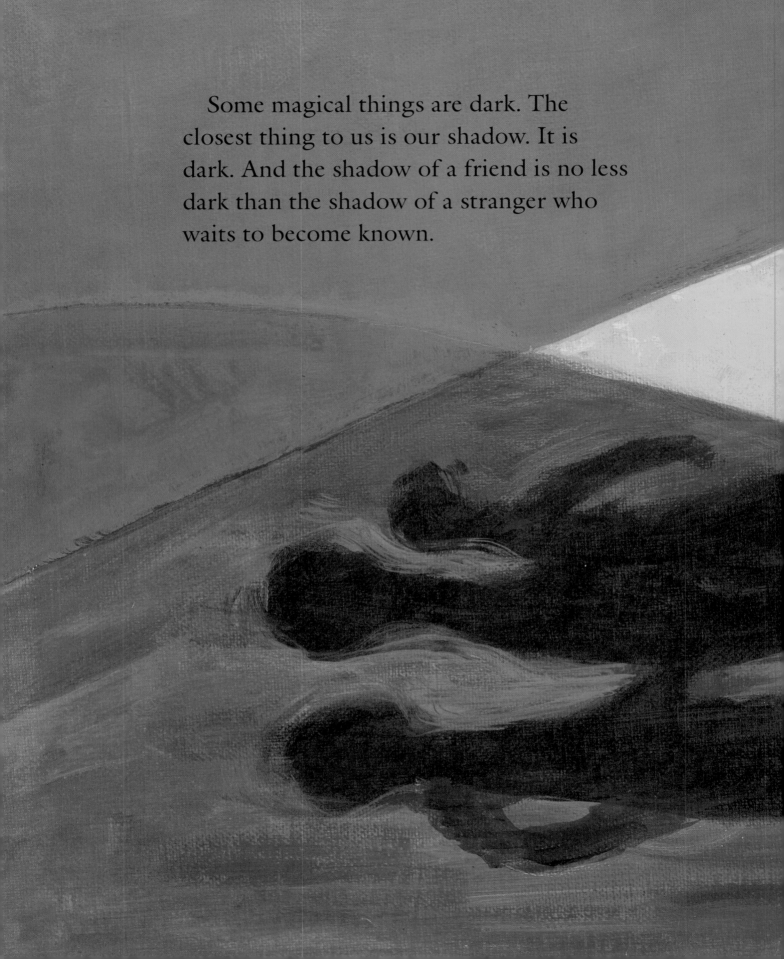

Some magical things are dark. The closest thing to us is our shadow. It is dark. And the shadow of a friend is no less dark than the shadow of a stranger who waits to become known.

The shade that welcomes the weary
is dark.
   Our most secret thoughts come from
the dark inside of our minds. Creativity
seeds there and grows into new ideas.

It is evening time, at the end of a busy day, when family and friends gather for laughter and talk.

Pale moonlight forms dark, shimmering silhouettes.

Quiet reigns in the deep darkness when the horizon is lost and heaven and earth become one. The darkest hour just before dawn is dreamtime.